DIGITAL EMPATHY

WHEN TECH MEETS TOUCH

MARCO GIANOTTEN

Amsterdam

Author: Marco Gianotten
Editor: Erik Bouwer
Project Manager and *digital native*: Tess van Genderen
Layout and illustrations: Overhaus, Amsterdam
Printing: Leijten, Amsterdam
Translation: Multitaal, Amsterdam
Yellow Suit: Opposuits

ISBN 978-90-825564-1-4
Copyright © 2017, Marco Gianotten, Giarte

For my children, Enzo, Boaz and Tirza, and all other *digital natives* from Generation Z. Along with Generation Y, they will form nearly three-fourths of the active workforce in companies and the public sector in 2025.

About the author

Marco Gianotten is the founder of Giarte. He's a writer, columnist and inspirational speaker. Marco and his team organize sessions and workshops on digital empathy and the rethinking of Enterprise IT. He's married and father to three teenagers.

About Giarte

Giarte is a data-driven advisory firm with a passion for simplification. Giarte helps companies to focus relentlessly on user experience and outside-in performance management.

www.giarte.com

BEHIND THE SCENES

The past years, I have advised businesses and inspired people to try a different approach to bogged-down IT projects and outsourcing relationships that they just can't seem to get off the ground: Look at them from the outside in, discover their true essence, and stop hiding behind processes and defending yourself with a "conditional yes" every time. At a certain point, visions and experiences will congeal into a new way of doing things. For me, that led to "inventing" the *eXperience Level Agreement* (XLA). For years now, my firm Giarte and I have been helping large companies grasp, measure, and improve IT. I had seen that the world of "soft data" was miles away from the world of financial and technical performance indicators. The process of bridging those worlds took me back to the drawing board, which is where I came up with the XLA. The past years, that idea was developed into an approach with workshops and tools for measurement and making improvements. More and more people kept asking when I was finally going to put that information together in a handy little book. So I took on that challenge with the help of my team at Giarte.

Marco Gianotten

CONTENTS

"Writing is easy, you just have to cross out the wrong words."

Mark Twain
1835 - 1910

DIGITAL EMPATHY

WHY THERE'S NO GETTING AWAY FROM IT

Ask a CEO what he or she lies awake at night thinking about and eliminate all the household problems (mortgage, kids, and parents). Chances are that "Can't keep up with the pace of change" will be somewhere at the top of the list. In this boardroom nightmare, the business model is brought down by a disruptive newcomer. This is all about advances in technology. IT not only forms the basis for nearly every existing business process, but it is also the deciding factor in an organization's speed and maneuverability. In other words, IT has gone from being a side issue to a major issue. Many a CEO feels the pressure: "We need to transform into a digital company!" At conferences and in the media, *disruption, exponential development,* and *digital transformation* are increasingly the leading topics.

But let's be honest. Most companies are not Uber, Google, Apple, or Airbnb – far from it. They are neither trendsetting nor agile. Disruptive, perhaps? Not by a long shot. Most companies just keep on toiling away every day in order to survive. Senior executives and CIOs of the larger organizations realize that it takes a lot of time and energy to keep IT systems up and running. After nearly half a century, many companies see IT as synonymous with a complex succession of generations of technology. Maneuverability and flexibility are not exactly the fortes of the average IT environment. That makes it difficult to keep pace with change – let alone make it through digital transformation unscathed. Why is this important? Because anyone who still wants to be around in ten years will need to change course: from the traditional shareholder value model to creating lasting customer value. A company's ability to differentiate itself lies not in more products but in services and the customer experience. As the economy goes increasingly digital, it will become ever more important to understand what drives customers, what makes employees successful, and what makes companies relevant. The key to success is *empathy*.

For an organization to clear all these hurdles, the business side and IT side need to work together as a seamless whole. That means sharing the same basic principles and goals as well as speaking the same language. Just as in any relationship, that calls for trust and respect. But people who work in the IT department of a large organization often hear their co-workers complain that they don't get the respect, esteem, or trust that they deserve. The low standing of IT inside the company stands in stark contrast to the increasing importance of new information technology to a company's right to exist. So what's going on here? Have IT professionals made it too difficult for the business organization to work with them? Yes. IT still often speaks a language that is incomprehensible to the rest of the organization. IT got away with that for quite a while, which is no big surprise given its internal monopoly on supplying the business organization with computerization. And in doing so, IT left its mark on systems, processes, and procedures – and on end users.

But it's all over as far as the IT monopoly is concerned. Willing or unwilling, business organizations are going their own way today. Cloud IT and mobile applications are major drivers behind *shadow* IT: systems and solutions that are acquired and applied beyond the IT organization's range. There are all kinds of risks to these under-the-radar actions by the business organization, which would make an outright ban seem like a logical response. The pressure and desire the business experiences to think digitally for itself only increases. The real reason for shadow IT goes much deeper: a lack of trust in IT.

Ask business managers what they really think of their IT organization and you can expect to hear words like "aloof," "slow," "over-detailed," "difficult," "stubborn," "incomprehensible," and "bureaucratic." Recurring experiences with unsuccessful IT projects and incidents define how managers see their IT organization. Trust has been betrayed in the other direction too. Ask IT professionals what they think of their business organization and they also have negative associations: "unrealistic," "nagging," "oblivious," "naive," and "condescending." When things go wrong in the business organization, people are quick to blame IT.

These mutual prejudices are demonstrative of a gap between the business organization and IT. When management says the company is on its way to becoming a tech company, it's time to give short shrift to the division between *us* (IT) and *them* (the rest of the company). That gap cannot be "repaired overnight" with a new process, trendy tools or a nifty program for business-IT alignment. For digital transformation, that gap has to be more than just narrowed: it needs to be closed. Change starts with you, by admitting that there's a gap and that it's a problem for you and the other side alike. To strengthen mutual trust, both sides need affective and cognitive skills: hearts and minds. The main ingredient for successful IT transformation is the development of *empathy*. Only then can the gap between the real world and the world of technology and processes be closed.

Marco Gianotten
Chief ~~Executive~~ Officer
Empathy

WHAT'S THE CHEAPEST INCIDENT TO RESOLVE?

*THE ONE THAT NEVER HAPPENED

"The secret of change is to focus all of your energy, not on fighting the old, but on building the new."

Socrates

_X - 399 BC_

CHAPTER 1

HEADING TOWARDS AN IT CRISIS?

In the movie *The Big Short*, actor Christian Bale shines in the role of hedge fund manager Michael Burry. His character correctly forecasts the eventual subprime mortgage crisis in 2008. How did he become so good at market speculation? It seems that Burry learned a lot from that other financial crisis, back in the 1930s. He says there were two signs at the time that the real estate bubble was about to burst. The first one was the complexity of the financial system: it had all become so convoluted that nobody knew which way was up anymore. And real criticism of the system was few and far between. With their blinders on, people also failed to see the second sign: the system had become so complex that cases of mortgage fraud were skyrocketing. These two things told hedge fund manager Michael Burry to go *short*: right before the latest financial crisis of 2008 erupted, he reaped enormous profits from speculating on the inevitable collapse of subprime mortgage funds.

One Trillion Dollars in Complexity

Stifling complexity and room to doctor the figures: that's the parallel to the status of IT in large corporations and government agencies. Since the Industrial Revolution, technological innovation has formed the basis for our increased prosperity and welfare. Then, half a century ago, information technology (IT) came along, and IT organizations were set up to steer computerization in the right direction. Since then, the pace of innovation has picked up from one decade to the next. Nowadays, nearly every business process has an IT system behind it, and large organizations sometimes have even thousands of applications to maintain. To get that complexity under control, IT departments have established scores of processes and procedures. Since the financial crisis of 2008, organizations have continued to cut their budget for preventative IT maintenance year by year. In 2010, the amount required to catch up on the overdue maintenance for software applications, known as IT *debt*, was estimated by Gartner at 500 billion dollars[1]. At the time, Gartner predicted that this amount would grow to one trillion dollars by 2015. Complexity is a fact, and IT organizations have no problem whatsoever with making it worse than it already is.

Unraveling IT: How It Thinks and Acts

By now, the IT landscape is more complex than ever before. In the quest for greater agility, business organizations are increasingly going their own way as they often bypass an internal IT organization that is busy trying to keep the boat afloat and therefore "can't be disturbed right now." Cloud IT, big data, and mobile applications are the main drivers behind the phenomenon of *shadow* IT: systems and solutions that are acquired and applied beyond the IT organization's range. The consequences: security, integration, and continuity risks, a lack of mutual trust between the business organization and IT, recurring experiences with unsuccessful projects, and incidents where IT is generally blamed.

Complexity, high costs, and a lack of trust: the pressure on IT is mounting. In the meantime, companies are increasingly dependent on the speed and agility of IT departments – providing stability and reliability alone no longer does the trick. It cannot be ruled out that the IT function in organizations may one day slowly grind to a halt, resulting in an IT *crisis* and, consequently, a call for IT transformation. So what's the deal with IT, and how can we prevent an IT crisis? For a proper analysis, we need to make sense out of how IT thinks and acts. And what better place to start than with our brain.

THE TWO SIDES OF OUR BRAIN

Our brain is our most complex organ, and it still holds many secrets – even for scientists. Our brain has two interconnected sides: the left and the right side. Logic, sequences, and analysis are the domain of the left-side. The right-side is more involved with emotional expression, creativity, and seeing things as a whole. We process new information with the left-side by first seeing the details and then putting that information into context. With the right-side, we do the exact opposite: first we see the whole and then the details. In spite of their specializations, both sides of the brain are equally developed, and both sides constantly communicate with each other. Many tasks require both sides of the brain to work together. For example, while producing speech and comprehending language are specializations of the left side, the right side of the brain is particularly good at processing intonation. When processing language, signals go back and forth through the *corpus callosum*, which connects both sides. Just how important this connection is can be judged from the research by Nobel Prize winners Roger Sperry and Michael Gazzaniga[2]. In the 1960s, they studied patients whose *corpus callosum* had been surgically split – as a last resort to treat epilepsy – and where the two sides of the brain could no longer communicate with each other. As a result, when these patients were given something to look at using just their left eye, they were no longer able to express verbally what they had seen. Images seen by the left eye are processed by the right side of the brain, while the language center is controlled by the left side.

Each Side Has Its Talents

A lot of research has been done on the functions controlled by each side of the brain and how both sides work together. Maurizio Zollo of the Massachusetts Institute of Technology (MIT) studied the brain activity of 63 managers and entrepreneurs[3]. When asked to perform *exploitation* tasks involving left-side functions like rational and logical thinking, like keeping a company running, the managers scored better. When asked to perform *explorative* tasks involving right-side creative and high-level thinking functions, like finding new ways to do things, the entrepreneurs scored better. The brain scans showed that when performing tasks to improve and find new ways to do things, both sides of the brain were engaged. When performing explorative tasks, however, heightened activity in the right side of the brain could only be seen among the entrepreneurs. This heightened activity in the right side of the brain is also seen in other processes conducted by our central nervous system. Researchers at Carnegie Mellon and MIT had 566 human test subjects perform tasks in groups[4]. The outcome was that teams with a higher collective EQ (Emotional Quotient) performed better. EQ is seen as the sum of characteristics such as social skills, the capacity for self-reflection, and humor: important traits for a good manager, which are also closely connected to the right side of the brain. So the entrepreneurs, while performing explorative tasks, were able to make more extensive use of their brains. This does not mean that entrepreneurs are smarter but that they are more engaged in rational **and** logical thinking.

What Makes for a Successful Leader?
In his book *Leaders Eat Last*[5], Simon Sinek does the math to show that masculine leaders like Jack Welch (CEO of General Electric from 1981 to 2001) are successful because of their *commanding* management style and focus on shareholder value while the *people-oriented* leadership of Jeff Sinegal (CEO of retailer Costco), for example, is much more productive in the long run. For most male leaders, however, Sinegal's style is more the exception than the rule. Non-executive directors, stock market analysts, headhunters and, senior managers have a preference for strong, dominant leaders. In times of uncertainty and change, we are apt to fall back on old patterns from the culture where we were raised and grew up. Characters like J.R. Ewing, the macho oil tycoon in prime-time U.S. television series *Dallas* from the 1980s, have fed our preconceptions with masculine leadership competencies. That prejudice trickles all the way down to a company's value and to punishing CEOs who show a soft side. When Ton Büchner in 2012, as the new head of paint and chemicals group AkzoNobel, took some time off due to fatigue, the company's market value plummeted by 600 million euros that same day. That extreme reaction was driven in part by our preconceptions about strong leadership. And those preconceptions are hard to shake.

THE DOMINANCE OF THE LEFT SIDE OF THE BRAIN

Using the left side of our brain has been overrated for quite some time now. During the Industrial Revolution, professions that hinged on rational thinking became much more prestigious. Technical professions were held in high esteem later in the twentieth century too: parents were delighted if a son or daughter wanted to become a doctor, engineer or pilot. For many years now, the work that is done in IT departments also emphasizes skills associated with the left side of the brain. Building and managing IT systems requires in-depth computer expertise and attention to detail. Software programmers need to be accurate workers because it's easy to make an error when entering machine code – and bugs often have major consequences.

The Binary Brain of IT

Just like machine code, the field of IT is also binary by nature. Something is either correct or incorrect; "approximately" does not work as a specification in IT. In the days that IT was about computerization on the basis of clear-cut specifications, the dominance of left-brain thinking was not a problem – on the contrary. For the first generation of computers and computer languages, people with a strong technical bent were needed to write programs and keep them running. No wonder that since their origin almost 45 years ago, IT departments have been literally *manned* (women are still highly underrepresented, even in IT management) by aging left-brainers.

In the 1970s, when computerization became increasingly important, IT departments started to grow. They became organizations within organizations, which were portrayed in the organizational chart as a support department alongside "normal" life in the company.

When Fortran and Cobol (the first programming languages) were introduced, that's when the initial divide in IT between development and management was made. In the course of time IT continued to grow, which made it necessary to become more specialized in tasks such as networking and project management. Starting in the 1980s, IT organizations then started dividing, contracting out, and outsourcing their service domains. Their hardware was supplied by vendor A, management by vendor B, and connectivity by vendor C. Business applications were built by vendor X, maintained by vendor Y, and hosted by vendor Z. Although initially a technical exercise, this segregation of duties definitely left its mark on the department's culture. Relationships with customers were laid down in long contracts and Service Level Agreements (SLAs). And in order to monitor the complex internal processes, IT departments started working with lots of technical Key Performance Indicators (KPIs), such as the average availability of servers and maximum delay of data traffic in a network. IT performance was charted in reports and score-cards, but its relationship to processes in the business organization and among end users was becoming increasingly muddled – just like with the relationships between the different specializations inside IT.

KPIs and Reality

The purpose of KPIs is to provide information, but because of them decision-makers can lose touch with reality. In the world of Fast Moving Consumer Goods (FMCG), product safety is a top priority. If a food and beverage company has issues with its food safety because of a problem in production, its reputation is at stake. Recalls are not

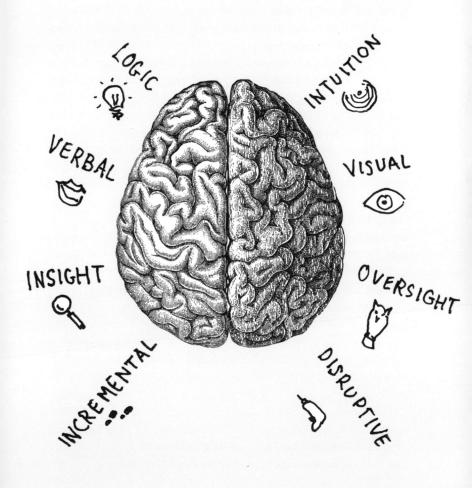

LOGIC

INTUITION

VERBAL

VISUAL

INSIGHT

OVERSIGHT

INCREMENTAL

DISRUPTIVE

good for a brand's image, which would make a KPI like "no recalls" logical. Or would such a KPI destroy an open safety culture? Food and beverage company Nestlé became involved in a long drawn-out lawsuit with a whistleblower, former Food Safety Manager Yasmine Motarjemi. She said that a repressive management culture, combined with bonuses for "no recalls", had led to downplaying incidents such as where babies had nearly choked when eating a baby cookie. With product safety, it is important how senior management reacts to anomalies in quality. Which is the deciding factor in that case: ethics or profits? "No recalls" is a noble KPI where internal operational excellence is concerned, but it does not do much good to the world outside.

By continuing to think along the lines of technology, numbers and details (hardware, network, software, and devices) instead of targeted business outcomes and productive end users (profit, success, impact), IT got more and more out of touch with the outside world. IT was mainly geared to keeping systems up and running; hardly any time was set aside for thinking about alternative ways of doing things. Are the services supplied by the IT department or external service provider helping the business or actually hurting it? In short, there was no connection between technology and day-to-day business.

THE OUTSIDE WORLD RATTLES THE DOORS OF IT
For quite some time, IT professionals had little cause to consider end users or the context of the organization. IT was run like the

engine room of a supertanker: all the machinery needed to be kept running smoothly. There was not much reason for the people in the engine room to know what was going on in the pilothouse: what is our course, what circumstances do we need to bear in mind, and what changes are on the horizon?

Consumers Expect More

Over the past ten years, technology and globalization have transformed the field of IT. First of all, consumers and employees (who are also consumers) expect more from the products and services supplied by companies. In their daily life, consumers make extensive use of cloud IT and mobile applications while having faith in the good intentions of the providers where their privacy and security are concerned. In e-commerce, long gone are the days when purchasing decisions were based on price. What's important today are all the services surrounding the product: a well-organized webstore providing clear information, fast delivery times, and a good returns policy. For banks, electronic banking is no longer a *unique selling point* but a *dissatisfier* if the online environment is prone to downtime. Companies that burden customers with IT processes that do not function properly – making trusted services unavailable – create an aversion avalanche on social media. Consumers have therefore taken a dominant position. *User experience*, *user interaction*, and *customer experience* are becoming the guiding principles for more and more companies in the development of new products and services. In *design thinking*, where innovation is achieved through co-creation, the focus is not only on the product or service but also on the customer experience. That increases the chance of commercial success. If the product is awkward, does not make things more convenient or fails to help solve a problem, that product will not be accepted, will not be embraced. "Start with the experience and work your way backwards to the technology", the mantra of Steve Jobs, is one of the basic principles of design thinking.

Experience Rules

In designing the interior of the Boeing 787 Dreamliner, psychologists were asked to determine what people wanted during a flight, even if they were unable to put that into words. "I want more legroom" is a no-brainer, but "I don't want to feel closed in" sounded strange to the aeronautical engineers coming from passengers who were prepared to sit in a closed tube at an altitude of more than 30,000 feet with an outside temperature of -58 Fahrenheit. Our sense of space is created mainly by our peripheral vision: what we can see outside our central field of view. Two illuminated arches over the width of the airplane have been incorporated into the Dreamliner's internal design. They carry the eye upwards and create the impression of more space than, for instance, in a Boeing 777 (which is actually bigger than the Dreamliner).

In his bestseller A Whole New Mind[6], Daniel Pink explains that in our changing world content is gradually taking a backseat to context, which is gaining in importance – also in sectors where innovation has traditionally been more technical by nature. When automotive company Porsche unveiled the Mission E, an all-electric concept car, in September 2015, the first thing they talked about was its emotional design. Only then did they move on to the car's excellent technical performance features. To make driving an electric car a success, the emotional experience of the design (right side of the brain) is at least as important as the car's environmental aspects and technical performance (left side of the brain).

New Rules, Different Pace

There is a second trend that should give traditional IT professionals a shake-up. It turns out − not for the first time − that established business models are vulnerable to disruptive newcomers. Sectors like financial services and the electric power industry can no longer rely on the status quo. A revenue model lasts only so long; once a competitor comes along who makes things more intelligent, faster or better for consumers, the model's time is up. Innovation no longer hinges on size, an established position or capital but on creativity, speed, and empathy. We have all heard of disruptive companies like Airbnb and Uber, but most companies are faced with the challenge of adapting on time and successfully to the digital world. This is about more than just keeping up with all the changes in the market. Cutting costs − so as to compete with newcomers without legacy systems − is also vital. The same goes for boosting reliability and security in order to protect the business organization from dangers from cyberspace and make it fully compliant with laws and regulations. The pressure on IT from the outside is enormous.

THE INSIDE WORLD OF IT

Not only the outside world but also the inside world of IT is changing. IT professionals and their bosses – the CIOs – have been given a lot to deal with over the past few years. They are up to their ears in work such as modernizing, combining, and integrating complex applications, sometimes as a result of a merger or acquisition. In addition, CIOs are being challenged to do more with less, while also being expected to get involved on time with new technologies such as cloud IT and mobile apps. In the meantime, outdated systems have to be kept up and running in a world of increasing security and privacy requirements.

There has been talk of simplifying complex application landscapes for more than a decade now. A solid effort was made to modernize the layers of technology under the business applications in recent years with the consolidation of networks, data centers, and platforms. Business application rationalization has generally been less successful, however. This is mainly because the business organization, as the owner of the business applications, is often unwilling to invest in their simplification and elimination. It prefers spending its money on functional changes and even more new systems. With IT, the emphasis has remained on standardization and automation, not elimination and simplification. As the infrastructure costs kept decreasing year by year – along with the total cost of IT – application rationalization often dropped off the list of priorities.

Not only is the stuff provided by the IT organization to support the business often outdated, but the *human capital* is also showing some cracks. Expertise in new systems and technologies is hard to come by; expertise in old systems is draining away. The average age of IT specialists at major corporations is higher than 50 years, and outsourcing (such as to low-wage countries) is also accountable for the departmental brain drain. The latter has inspired various major corporations to pool and update their expertise in old core systems and programming languages. Rabobank has started training a new generation of payment professionals in order to retain expertise in important core systems. Following suit with companies like General Motors and General Electric, Shell is working towards four strategic IT hubs (Houston, London, Rijswijk, and Bangalore), where IT work focusing on development, projects, and changes will be performed and operations will be outsourced. IT will be tackled in chains, and business clusters, such as oil extraction and distribution. That too, should provide a solution to the growing knowledge problem.

The Nature of IT Is Also Changing

Outsourcing and technological advancement also have an effect on the content of the work performed by IT professionals. As the quality of application development continues to improve thanks to new methods and tools, less code needs to be debugged. The underlying IT infrastructure is being virtualized, its *deployment* industrialized. Manual processes are playing less and less of a role. The clear organizational line in IT between development and management is gradually fading away as development and operations continue to be automated. These were traditionally two separate worlds, each with its own culture and dynamics. *DevOps* brings these worlds together, but that calls for new collaboration and communication skills. By contrast, other IT tasks are gradually being automated away. While

E-COMMERCE'S LEFT BRAIN ON OUTAGES

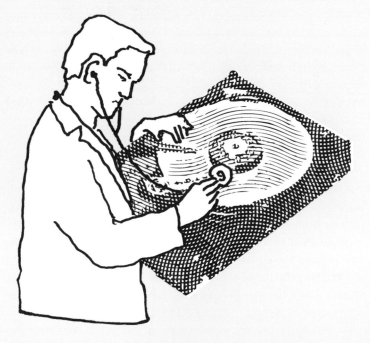

THE AMOUNT OF TIME ALLOWED
FOR A SYSTEM TO BE RECOVERED AND
FULLY FUNCTIONAL

E-COMMERCE'S RIGHT BRAIN ON OUTAGES

THE AMOUNT OF DATA THAT CONSUMERS ARE WILLING TO LOSE IN THE EVENT OF A RECOVERY

an average of two hours a month was still spent on managing a server in 2005, this had already been reduced to less than ten minutes in 2015. This places the functional management of IT increasingly in the hands of the business organization.

In the coming years, many traditional jobs in IT, such as infrastructure managers, testers, and database administrators, will disappear. On the other hand, the jobs that remain and the new ones created will require an increasingly higher level of education and other competencies. The professionals needed today and tomorrow need to be adept in modifying, replacing, and phasing out older applications that pose a risk in complex chains so that incidents can be kept to a minimum. IT professionals will also need to learn how to deal with vertical responsibilities across chains: right through the traditional layers of applications, middleware, data centers, and networks.

The IT End User Is a Consumer

In addition, the IT organization is also faced with end users of IT systems who have different requirements than before. In daily life, IT end users are simply consumers who make extensive use of the latest technology. Just like other consumers, they want to work with handsome and well-designed products and user-friendly software; not only because they expect greater added value and ease-of-use but also because they have become more dependent for their own productivity on effective IT that performs well. IT also needs to fit in seamlessly with individual styles of working and learning curves as well as the rapidly changing needs arising from the business.

Vice versa, poorly designed products and services can lead to extra expenses because of the longer learning curve when rolling out new releases and functionalities for example. Besides the loss of productivity, this can also lead to more questions for trainers and help desk personnel. User-unfriendly solutions also necessitate more workarounds and shadow IT.

IT TRYING TO FIND ITS WAY IN THE NEW WORLD

A new economic reality, tougher competition, critical consumers, and demanding end users: factors that are forcing IT to fundamentally change how it works. Not inside out, but outside in. Instead of prioritizing the process, it's all about the needs of the people who keep the business organization running as it grows and develops. In essence, IT needs to be simpler and faster, and do more to make the company strong and maneuverable.

Luckily, CIOs and their teams have not been sitting around doing nothing for the past few years. They have made a lot of changes towards the business organization and customers as well as towards IT end users. Great strides have been made in system development and how management and service processes are designed. As the quality of application development continues to improve thanks to new methods and tools, less needs to be debugged. The underlying IT infrastructure is being virtualized, the rollout of applications industrialized. Through the introduction of DevOps, more and more companies are seeing the traditional division between development and management – once separate worlds, each with its own culture and dynamics – gradually disappear. By installing iterative, small, and well-tested releases, they can minimize the risks associated with change. In agile software development, the product owner is part of the team, and user stories occupy center stage. Agile also fits in with the push for more right-brain thinking in IT.

We benefit every day from what the CIOs have done for us as consumers. We don't have to go to the bank anymore to manage our finances, and thanks to online travel agencies we can plan and book a trip from the comfort of our own home. For their IT end users, CIOs have set up self-service portals, implemented Bring Your Own Device (BYOD) policies, and opened IT service centers for employees with a *look and feel* on a par with Apple's Genius Bar. These are all excellent initiatives that fit in well with how the right side of the brain works: "What is the effect and how does it feel?"

User Brain Damage or Real Understanding?
So it seems that the business organization and IT have been narrowing the gap. In the past two decades, a lot of energy has been put into building bridges between IT and the business organization – consultants have earned a fortune with solutions for business-IT alignment. IT listens better, has a better understanding of what the business organization wants, has adapted certain working procedures, and is more oriented towards end users. But no matter how busy IT has been, many of these changes are mainly cosmetic. IT still clings to its old introspective and bureaucratic ways. As a result, the old core remains untouched and dominated by left-brain thinking.

A glance at an IT organization's innovation agenda is all it takes to see that IT naturally gravitates more towards hardware and software than innovations that are advantageous for the rest of the company. Trends like *software defined networking* and *hyper-converged infrastructure* make many an IT professional's heart beat faster. But is that also what the business organization needs? IT professionals still fail to fully comprehend that users don't read manuals anymore; they just call the help desk, which sees their questions as proof of "user brain damage." IT professionals are still unable to deliver new systems in accordance with specifications – and then they wonder why end users complain. IT professionals are content with SLAs in the form of bronze, silver, and gold availability rates that they conclude with external vendors, while the business organization is looking for a reasonable balance between risk and costs. If business-critical IT systems fail, the right side of management's brain is suddenly engaged in a fit of anger against the mess created by a serious incident. If someone from IT then responds from the left side of their brain that "they were just following ITIL processes," that only adds fuel to the fire. Users are pissed off about the problem, and puzzled about the solution. Put these two words together and you get "pizzled": an extremely negative emotion often evoked by IT.

IN SEARCH OF BALANCE IN IT'S BRAIN

Even though the gap between IT and the business organization is only organizational, there is a mental side to it as well. IT professionals have a hard time thinking about the context, the circumstances, and the end users. And to be perfectly honest, the business organization finds it difficult to think about the importance of a company-wide IT approach and to accept the consequences of its own activities and projects. Do companies suffer from a "split brain?" And is it all over for left-brainers in IT? No. In managing different IT and other processes, companies still benefit from professionals who are good at following procedures. In some cases, it is even a disadvantage if someone is continually caught up in the context instead of the process itself. Many jobs in IT are still cut out for – and attractive to – left-brainers. A sharp focus, attention to detail and feeling comfortable with repetitive work are traits that still make for a good software tester.

Who Wants to Survive?
Yet dealing successfully with change calls for sensitivity, maneuverability, and flexibility. In order to survive, you need to be alert (observe) and adjust well to changing conditions (act). Seeing the context, the chains in which you form a link, the big picture: now that's what the right side of our brain is good at. But only if given the room to do so, even when processes are not completely predictable or under complete control. IT professionals achieve little through the old, systematic left-brain thinking. Techies have to be good with technology, but they also require an understanding of people, behavior, context, and dynamics. In short, IT professionals need to strike a new balance. And CIOs have to realize they need a well-balanced team to tackle the challenges that IT departments will face. That means being open to right-brain thinking and doing.

"We can't solve problems by using the same kind of thinking we used when we created them."

Albert Einstein
1879 - 1955

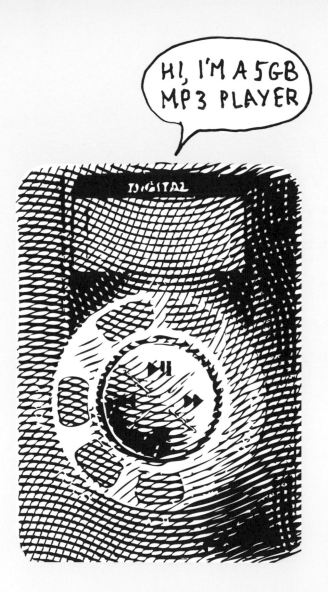

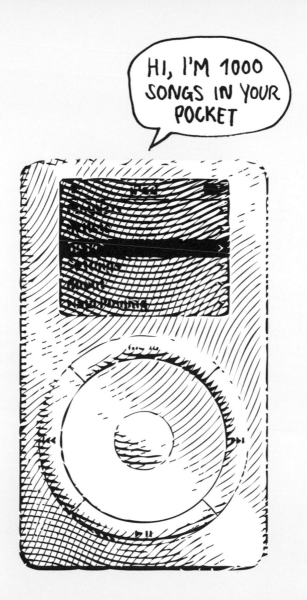

"Simplicity is the ultimate sophistication."

Leonardo da Vinci
1452 – 1519

CHAPTER 2

THE INGREDIENTS OF IT — NEW STYLE

Henri Mintzberg, one of the most widely read academics on management, unerringly puts his finger on the bureaucratic characteristics shared by organizations. Compared to the marvel of being able to fly from one continent to the other, he goes through the inimitable processes of air travel in his book *Why I Hate Flying*[7]. "Airlines are masters at changing cattle into sardines. If you want to fly somewhere, you must begin by being herded – in and out, back and forth, up and down. You stand in line to get a boarding pass to replace the ticket they just sold you. Then you stand in line to show your boarding pass to prove you bought the ticket they just took away from you. After this you stand in line to give back the boarding pass they just gave you." A lot has changed in our economy, technology, and even in aviation since Mintzberg's book first came out. The Boeing 787 Dreamliner may have been designed with the latest concepts in mind, but most airline companies (and airports) still have a lot to learn about the new era in which companies need to embrace customer awareness and maneuverability. Customer awareness: so they can observe the market they serve and how people around them behave. Maneuverability: so they can quickly change course, strategy or even their entire revenue model.

Organization: A Group of People

Are customer awareness and maneuverability characteristics of organizations or of the people who work there? An organization's success depends in part on empathetic leaders who are capable of adapting, making effective use of talented people in their organization and are aware of their customers and market. Seeing the context, the chains that your organization is part of, and keeping the big picture in mind: now that's what the right side of our brain is good at. That is also the weak point of IT organizations, where the emphasis lies on micromanagement and detailed planning – typical of left-brain thinking. What arrangements do IT departments make with their partners? What tools do they use, and do they adapt them as circumstances dictate? What's the use of carrots and sticks in encouraging teamwork? And what's to be gained with openness and transparency? In this chapter we go into the building blocks of collaboration and how IT deals with them.

Successful Collaboration

An organization is a group of people with a common goal. It sounds simple, but miles and miles of management books have been written about business management, groups, people, and goals. This gives the impression that the operation of an organization is quite a job. Luckily there's also a bright side. Simon Sinek illustrates in his book *Start with Why*[8] how the four ingredients for personal happiness apply to the corporate world, organizations, and leadership. The way we act is driven by chemicals in our brain: hormones and neurotransmitters. Endorphins are painkillers that are released when we put stressful situations into perspective with humor. Dopamine is released, for instance, when we enjoy ourselves – such as when we achieve goals. Two other substances, serotonin and oxytocin, play a role in social relations. Serotonin is released when we achieve success, and oxytocin is a hormone that is released when we feel connected and act not only out of self-interest. In *Leaders Eat Last*, the sequel to *Start with Why*, Sinek also points out the risks of endorphins and dopamine: they are addictive and increase the chance of repeated behavior, even if that behavior is no longer necessary. That's when behavior becomes dysfunctional. As far as Sinek is concerned, successful collaboration mainly lifts our spirits. That is good news, because IT organizations can certainly use some of that positive energy. What's more, collaboration is exactly what IT organizations need in order to take the next step.

COLLABORATION? LET'S PUT THAT IN A CONTRACT!

In essence, collaboration is very simple and can be kicked off right away. Nevertheless, collaboration does not always turn out all right. First of all, we need to understand that "collaboration" is an abstract concept. And that's where the danger lies: people usually don't respond to abstract concepts with action, while action is exactly what collaboration requires. All you need to get a collaboration going is – initially – shared ideas or concepts. That takes a bit of coordination and the ability to see the big picture: the final result. It's not just about the goal but also about both sides' understanding of how they will work together – about communication, respect, trust, openness, and honesty. About responsibility, but also about customer awareness and the willingness to adapt. Once they decide to set all these things down in rules, procedures, agreements (SLAs), and measurable objectives (KPIs), there's a greater chance of collaboration getting bogged down. All sorts of things can go wrong when collaborating, but there is no such thing as a contract that can prevent them from happening, let alone a contract that can be used to improve collaboration. Collaboration is not the same thing as talking to a business manager about a project or integrating two applications. It is a relationship between people. Nevertheless, when CIOs decide to work with a new vendor, for instance, they often spend tons of money on the legal side. Yet whether the partners in that relationship "click": we still see that as something that happens (or not) by magic.

Rules of Collaboration

Collaboration in IT outsourcing is complex, and we like having clear rules and arrangements to fall back on. Most providers of IT services and their customers put these rules and arrangements down in writing in a Service Level Agreement (SLA). On the surface, SLAs seem to fit in well with the preferred style of the left side of our brain, but recently it seems that those SLAs are not as well adapted to daily practice. It appears that with each new generation of outsourcing, the contracts just keep getting longer, with more and more penalty clauses, to boot. All the while, the number of IT projects that fall short of expectations or overshoot the budget (in time or money) are certainly not on the decline. So the question is, what have we achieved with those increasingly long contracts? Giarte regularly receives lengthy contracts with the request to help make them easier to enforce. To make the terms of their business relationships more tangible, people like to set them down in writing. But what do we expect of a doctor, air traffic controller or judge? Certainly not only that they are capable and knowledgeable, but also that they can make a decision as a professional and as a human being if circumstances dictate. That makes trust an important condition for innovation and improvement. And the other way around, if there is a lack of trust there will be less willingness to make decisions, experiment, and

NUMBER
OF PAGES

FIRST SLA LAW

PROBABILITY IT
IS GOOD

innovate. Which is completely understandable, for the chance of being punished for mistakes is simply too great.

Carrots and Sticks

In many outsourcing contracts, the SLA is an expression of ingrained mistrust. Neither the outsourcer nor the service provider has a crystal ball; so instead, they try to avoid as many uncertainties as possible. The longer the contract, the greater the false sense of security: the future simply cannot be guaranteed. And the more detailed the contract, the more people will work on the basis of those details. While this is how IT professionals like to work (left-brain thinking), the problem is that they don't see the big picture. After all, the purpose of an SLA is to support collaboration: a right-brain process.

An important part of an SLA covers the use of "carrots and sticks." Burrhus Frederic Skinner, one of the foremost research psychologists of the twentieth century, discovered that we can strengthen our behavior with operant conditioning: rewarding increases the chance of desired behavior, and punishing decreases the chance of undesired behavior[9]. Later studies have continued to show that new behavior is easier to learn with carrots than with sticks. The down-side of the reward model (with the reward coming from outside) is that it decreases intrinsic motivation. In organizations, carrots and sticks are often connected to the achievement of goals or KPIs, but where collaboration is concerned, carrots and sticks certainly have some disadvantages.

First of all, the criteria for carrots and sticks are not always clear-cut in such situations. When using traditional goals such as "aggregate bandwidth" or "average resolution time," there is just too much room for discussion: is it about whether the supplier is technically in the right ("KPI A-Okay") or how the customer feels about the service ("still not satisfied")? These are "watermelon" SLAs: on the face of things all the supplier's meters light up green, but in reality everything is red (in the experience of the customer or end user). Organizations will be better off when they trade their watermelons for kiwis: they are small, and they are green on the outside, **and** on the inside.

When KPIs lack a clear relation to daily business (the context), that also makes them harder to judge. Take KPIs for availability for instance. An availability rate of 99.9 percent generally costs twice as much as an availability rate of 99.5 percent. What is actually the most appropriate rate depends in part on risk estimates and economic factors. But in daily practice – or during contract negotiations – it is usually the budget that rules, while the context is what is really needed to determine risk appetite. What is the effect on the business organization if that 0.1 percent unavailability materializes? At what times is its negative impact the greatest? *Downtime* in the form of a rate says nothing about the real economic impact – the amount of lost revenue or number of incomplete transactions does.

Risk Appetite

Carrots and sticks work pretty well for clear-cut tasks, but they are less effective for creative work and problem-solving. Of course it sounds attractive and fair to reward people for good results. In his book *Swimming with Sharks*[10], Joris Luyendijk says that over-rewarding encourages people to take too many risks. The Wall Street tenet of "the higher the incentive, the better the results" no longer holds. Put into IT terms: a large bonus for the bid team does not result in a better contract, because intrinsic motivation is not structurally influenced by financial reward. Yet intrinsically motivated employees are exactly what organizations need.

The effect of penalizing also has its limits. Financial penalties for failing to meet KPIs are rarely productive. The reason for the penalty is usually contested, and it's often easy to pin the failure on external factors so the supplier cannot be held overall accountable. In other cases, the penalty is paid and then slyly "recharged" to a different cost item as extra work. Severe penalties for repeated non-compliance with KPIs do not lead to better service. By that point everyone can probably forget the contract being extended. The damage has already been done.

Counterproductive Behavior
Finally, the use of reward and punishment can encourage different kinds of undesired behavior. In a culture where carrots and sticks play a leading role, employees will settle for just staying in the margins. In other words, avoiding the *stick* is often more attractive than accepting the *carrot*. This creates a culture where entrepreneurship and high performance are curbed. Besides counterproductive KPIs, there are also perverse KPIs that can pose a real threat. These are KPIs where meeting the performance criteria is more important

than providing the actual service. A good example is how the Dutch Railroad (NS) deals with train delays. It "cancels" them (scraps them from the timetable and therefore from the statistics) because the government will fine them if trains are delayed too often. Similar forms of calculating behavior can also be seen in IT service relationships. Meeting expectations with pressure from the outside, such as with a bonus or penalty driving extrinsic motivation, breeds passivity. Yet an environment full of changes and interdependencies calls for IT professionals who take the initiative and are able to think for themselves: inquisitive self-starters.

Command and Control Doesn't Work Anymore

Trying to cram collaboration into a contract full of rules: that's how the IT organization and the business organization, but also the IT organization and IT service providers, try to organize their marriage. Besides the pitfall of SLAs and KPIs, as explained above, this approach also lacks the other conditions for successful collaboration. In order to create a common objective with shared responsibility, it's not enough just to reach agreement on the individual goals of the working relationship. If you expect final results at the top of the organizational pyramid, you need more than just *command and control* from the top down. In the first place, collaboration means working together, in other words: the relationship as the starting point. Collaboration becomes more effective if there is trust and all partners are aware of each other and their market and are willing to adapt. These three factors are actually closely connected. They can be seen in organizations where there is room for social innovation, such as by embracing the agile method and working in scrum teams.

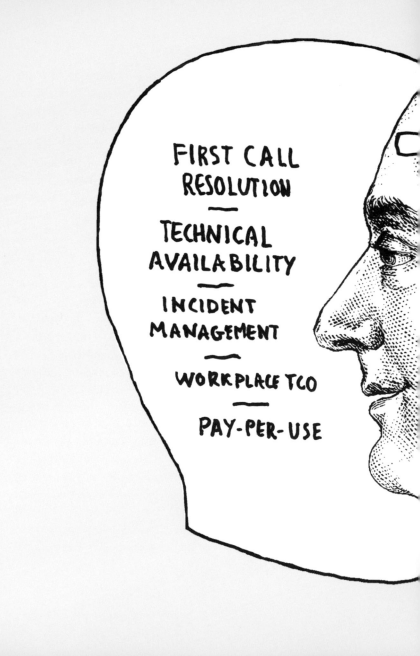

FIRST CALL
RESOLUTION
—
TECHNICAL
AVAILABILITY
—
INCIDENT
MANAGEMENT
—
WORKPLACE TCO
—
PAY-PER-USE

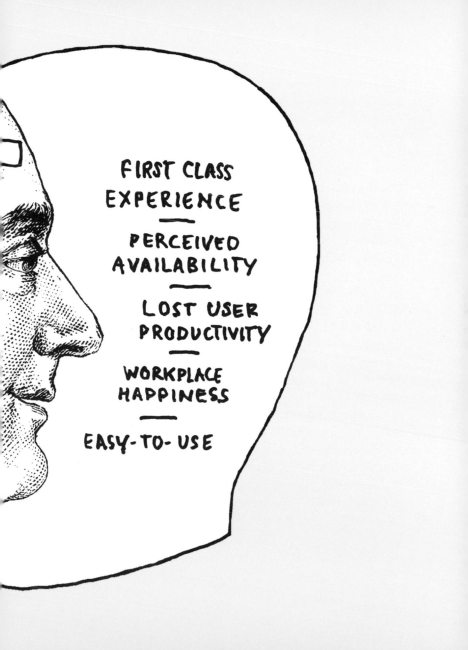

FIRST CLASS
EXPERIENCE
—
PERCEIVED
AVAILABILITY
—
LOST USER
PRODUCTIVITY
—
WORKPLACE
HAPPINESS
—
EASY-TO-USE

Intrinsically motivated IT professionals also need to have enough leeway on an individual level: independence to arrange their work themselves, take initiatives, and therefore adapt to the circumstances, and the context.

COLLABORATION CALLS FOR OPENNESS

Few experiences are as valuable as making a mistake. Yet most organizations have a culture with too high of a threshold for reporting problems and mistakes. This makes it quite a task to become a learning organization. But the advantages of becoming one are obvious: if you discover where things go wrong earlier on, you learn faster and can avoid problems, escalations, and unnecessary cost increases. The principle that made aviation as safe as it is today is called a *just culture*. This means that the organization creates a culture where people feel safe reporting mistakes and *near-misses* so they can be shared, discussed, and analyzed. The primary objective is to learn from mistakes. In aviation this starts with the assertion "I'm fit to fly" before going through the checklists. The principle of crew resource management – a variation on the four-eyes principle from corporate governance – has also done a lot of good. If one of the two pilots is not comfortable with a decision, that decision is simply rejected, no matter who in the cockpit has more authority. Companies from other sectors see the added value of these principles from aviation, and have started using them.

For instance, Rabobank is working towards a culture where mistakes and incidents form the basis for improvement. At face value, quick solutions to IT problems are exactly what the regulators want: financial institutions need to know and control the risks, and have established procedures to mitigate them. In the IT systems at banks, being *in demonstrable control* is converted into checklists, processes and procedures. In the event of a major incident, for example, a MIR (Major Incident Report) is required within 48 hours. Most mistakes and incidents – also major incidents – at the bank are almost always the result of human error. By looking at the airline industry (where roughly 80 percent of what goes wrong is due to human error), Rabobank knows that disasters are almost always preceded by a series of small incidents. That also includes a considerable number of *near-misses*. Inside the bank, these near-misses in IT were not reported in the past. The focus was on the heroes who saved the day instead. In an open culture, however, mistakes and incidents form the basis for improvement. As far as Rabobank is concerned, a change in culture starts at the top and with the management. But talking about a new culture is not enough. The point is to alter people's behavior: people must be willing and able to take responsibility. That requires a safe environment, where senior management sets a good example.

Right Side of the Brain: Seeing the Context
How do you escape from the daily pressure of dashboards and make sure that your work is about more than just going through checklists? It takes a lot to get IT professionals out of their comfort zone. But sometimes IT partners are just as intransigent, which makes collaboration difficult. A good fit between teams means more

for successful collaboration than a solid contract. The collaboration between airline company KLM and IT service provider Schuberg Philis illustrates this. KLM turns over millions of euros through online channels such as Facebook. On Facebook, KLM has more friends than any other airline in the world. Nearly one-fifth of all interaction with customers takes place on smartphones and tablet computers. During World Deal Weeks, one of KLM's sales campaigns, approximately two million emails are sent out within a couple of hours. KLM needs to be able to rely on flawless IT that can handle peak loads, with minimal latency between websites on every continent. All these Internet services call for not only an extremely maneuverable infrastructure but also smooth collaboration. The collaboration between KLM and Schuberg Philis is laid down in a Master Service Agreement (MSA), but that document is just three pages long and has not been altered in eleven years. The MSA provides a general outline for the individual SLAs for each project, which specifies the terms of collaboration. For KLM, it is not the KPIs or SLAs that determine the quality of collaboration. Instead, success is a matter of taking prompt and effective action. That also includes thinking ahead, offering help, and conferring. Not only outsourcer KLM, but also provider Schuberg Philis places high demands on collaboration. Projects that are not up to Schuberg Philis's quality standards lead to a discussion with KLM so that marketers understand what needs to be done to improve their quality. KLM and Schuberg Philis also regularly arrange "IT safaris" where new KLM marketers and campaign leaders get a crash course in "IT for non-IT professionals." That helps them understand what goes on over on the shop floor in IT. Campaign leaders who have not taken the course are simply not allowed to launch campaigns.

THE BEST KPIs ARE ABOUT THE ACTUAL BUSINESS

Shared responsibilities and a good view of the impact of IT processes on business operations, and vice versa, ensure that left-brain thinking can move more into the background. That starts with getting a feel for the context. Sometimes that means overcoming resistance. For example, IT organizations need to learn to keep traditional KPIs mainly to themselves (for internal use only). On the other hand, KPIs with a direct connection to the company's business organization can be very attractive. To illustrate, airline company KLM uses the KPI *Delayed Flights Due to IT*, and temp agency Randstad has come up with *Red Mondays* for processing the weekly time sheets where delays of more than 15 minutes make the day turn "red." In the event of a priority-one incident at online retailer bol.com, people are not allowed to go home until the problem is solved. A KPI for the maximum number of P1s (Priority One) is no longer used at bol.com.

Shared responsibilities and customer awareness come to the fore the most when – also with IT incidents – the economic impact on the business is taken into consideration, such as the number of customers affected or the amount of sales lost. There is another big advantage to KPIs geared to the business side: they enable the IT organization to conclude a "moral SLA" with the business organization.

Context-Based Collaboration: How?

There's nothing as hard as trying to unlearn something. That goes for SLAs too. They are a fact of life, and while they may not be perfect they still give us something to hold on to. Increasing control by relinquishing control: that's not exactly natural for IT managers.

The term *outcome-based performance* is a fancy way of saying what it's really all about: the outcome for the business organization. Experience is also part of that outcome. In the "new style" of SLAs, the outcome for the business organization occupies center stage. The next chapter shows which parts of the provision of IT services can be improved when a Service Level Agreement (SLA), based on numbers, is converted into an eXperience Level Agreement (XLA). And how to get from an SLA to an XLA.

"The wisdom of life consists in the elimination of non-essentials."

Lin Yutang
1895 – 1976

TRADITIONAL IT

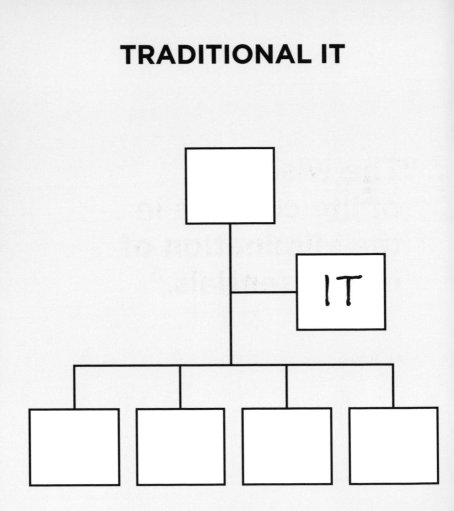

DIGITAL BY DEFAULT

"People will forget what you said, people will forget what you did, but people will never forget how you made them feel."

Maya Angelou
1928 - 2014

CHAPTER 3

EXPERIENCE FIRST WITH THE XLA

In his popular blog *The Number One Job Skill in 2020*[11], Forbes journalist George Anders points out the growing number of jobs in the US economy where empathy is the primary job requirement. School psychologists, music teachers, language and speech pathologists, personal financial planners, and private chauffeurs: jobs that are expected to grow by at least 20 percent. Technology makes anything and everything possible says Anders. We can use it to measure blood sugar levels or test a child's math skills. But the magic really happens when someone with diabetes or a grade school kid gains more self-confidence and becomes happier. In many cases, technology remains a measuring instrument. To understand the world around us better and tackle human issues and problems, it's not so much technology but empathy that we really need.

As far as I am concerned, reinventing IT in large organizations also starts with empathy. Since the birth of Giarte in 1994, I've talked to CIOs and business managers thousands of times. A lot of those discussions were about outsourcing and potential partnerships. Almost always, the issue or problem was not due to the phenomenon of outsourcing, but instead to the way IT professionals themselves work: collaboration, processes, and procedures, their view on IT services, and their vision for IT outsourcing. In the heyday of IT outsourcing, the contracts were mainly about how the service provider and the client IT organization were supposed to work together. Service levels were negotiated by the IT organization, not by the real customers on the business side. The end users – the business organization, so also the employees who depend on all that hardware and software – were hardly involved in the negotiations, if at all. IT as a department was too blind to the impact of IT, which today goes to the core of the business organization, and is constantly changing, to boot. On the contrary, the world of business IT is still dominated by SLAs that shine at excessive left-brain thinking.

It's my personal mission to solve the problems with SLAs and KPIs in IT services. I want to help make IT organizations more successful by getting them to work towards the final result. But how do you minimize the difference between what drives IT and what's really the most important thing for the success of the business? How do you close the gap between business and IT? To make the change from left-brain thinking to a more balanced orientation – where the business organization and end users occupy center stage – it is crucial to understand what goes on inside the business organization. What do end users (who are increasingly dependent on IT) have to deal with? Why do they cry "It doesn't work" without providing any details to explain what goes wrong? Why do primary emotions play such a large role in incidents? Why is the learning curve so steep when launching new business applications? It's high time for users to take center stage in everything that IT does and for these kinds of issues to be leading in how IT organizations operate. There's only one way to prioritize the experience of the end users, and that's by embedding that experience in the IT department's provision of service. That requires a new contract between IT and the business organization. In this chapter I show how you can get started on this new way of thinking and acting. As a counterbalance to the world of "left-brain SLAs" with their strong focus on process models and technical ratios: enter the XLA (eXperience Level Agreement).

WHAT IS AN XLA?

Before I continue, I want to give a few warnings. An XLA is neither a product nor a service nor a model. Neither is it a mechanism, agreement, document, process, procedure nor a way of working. The same goes for Agile and DevOps. These, too, are basic principles, ways of seeing things, and ways of thinking. Therefore, an XLA is not something you can implement or carry out. If that's the approach you take, the result will be a letdown. The same disillusion is what you get if you think all SLAs can be replaced by XLAs. SLAs are still needed, but they lack a connection to the outside world. By contrast, an XLA can be used to build a bridge between soft and hard KPIs and between hard data and human relations.

An XLA is an approach that focuses on business impact and user experience, and leads to a new, concrete way of thinking, doing, measuring and reporting. It's a work in progress with a growing number of best practices, showing that the approach produces a desired and proven result. An SLA is a contract; an XLA a commitment. An SLA is an effect of reason; an XLA creates the right balance by adding context and emotion. Where an SLA is a static thing, a file full of paper, an XLA (once put down in writing, and in just a few pages) is a dynamic document that can always be changed. Working with an XLA assumes a continuing process of measurement, analysis, and improvement. An added advantage is that an XLA can lead to simpler SLAs and the elimination of unnecessary complexity in rules and arrangements. Is an XLA only suitable for IT? No, an XLA can work as a catalyst for other *corporate functions* such as human resources, facilities management, finance, and procurement in order to focus on the customers of those services – and not the processes or the provider of the service.

DESIGN THINKING

More and more CIOs see the importance of a different way of working and running their IT organizations: in the design and management of functionality and in providing the related services, users and usability need to come first. But how do you make that happen? After years of working on the basis of technical performance, it's not easy to make room for subjective indicators and affective skills. Usability, like minimizing the difference between what the designer intends and what the user experiences, is difficult to capture in a scorecard. In the creative industry, *design thinking* is an effective way to tackle "the problem of problem-solving." Design thinking is all about observation and creating ideas. The goal is to come up with a better design for a product or service that truly meets the needs of the end user. That user can be a customer, but also an employee. What are the elements of design thinking that contribute to success?

- Learn to think outside the box. Nothing is impossible; keep asking why and don't take a "conditional yes" for an answer and you will widen your outlook.
- Put customer experience and emotional needs first, instead of technical characteristics.
- Instead of just one, go for multiple solutions where the characteristics of the best solutions are gradually selected and combined for a better final result.

Why am I such a fan of design thinking? It's a great approach to avoiding the traditional pitfalls of problem-solving. Give IT managers an issue, and the first thing they want to do is identify the problem so they can solve it right away. That is very bold and decisive of them, but managers in that mode of action are mainly concerned

HIGH TECH

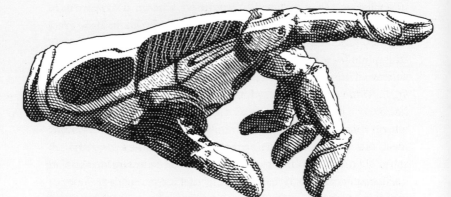

SOFTWARE DEFINED NETWORKING
HYPER-CONVERGED DATA CENTERS
ADAPTIVE SECURITY ARCHITECTURE
ADVANCED LAYER MANUFACTURING
AUTONOMOUS INTERNET OF THINGS
NEUROMORPHIC ARCHITECTURE
QUANTUM COMPUTING

HIGH TOUCH

INTUITIVE LEARNING
CONTEXT-DRIVEN PERSONALIZATION
EMOTIONAL DESIGN
TAILORED EXPERIENCE
MOTIVATIONAL STRATEGY
INTRINSIC MOTIVATION
SOCIAL RETURN

with the same old variables, and generally proceed the same old way. IT organizations are not naturally inclined to put users first, while that would be the most natural and practical solution for the issue of business-IT alignment.

Albert Einstein said: "We can't solve problems by using the same kind of thinking we used when we created them." So IT needs to find a new approach. Sometimes it's exactly the established frameworks and structures that limit the number of solutions. And at the outset, lots of good ideas are often shot down because they are fragile and less natural options. Sometimes concepts and new principles need a little more time to mature.

RETHINKING

Although there is no exact definition of design thinking, that does not stop companies from applying it successfully. Of course there are gurus who make away with it and try to turn design thinking into a model. But no single company has ever benefited from just applying a model. What's more important is the underlying idea, the conviction that a different way of seeing things or alternative approach is needed. We call this "rethinking." A good example of rethinking is something The American Book Center in Amsterdam tried. One of its employees decided to free up a special shelf in the store with a conspicuous sign: "Books Nobody Reads." Books were placed on that shelf that had been overlooked by the critics and for which there was no marketing budget. Not only did the designation "Books Nobody Reads" grab people's attention, but it also aroused their curiosity. The books from that shelf suddenly sold better than before, and the book store even made the newspaper with this creative solution. It's not only a "different way of thinking" that makes design thinking an attractive approach (important because IT professionals tend to engage mainly the left side of their brain); it also gives them something to hold on to by putting the end user first.

For developing its Genius Bar, Apple drew inspiration from the Ritz-Carlton hotel chain. The Ritz-Carlton concierge desk formed the source of inspiration for a place where well-trained, understanding personnel are there for guests with one single goal: answering questions and solving problems, hassle-free. Medical engineer Doug Dietz, who works for General Electric, has also mastered the art of rethinking. To kids, an MRI scanner is one big scary thing: it looks like a narrow tunnel that you have to crawl into, it makes noise, and you are not allowed to move. Saying "There's nothing to be afraid of" does not work very well, but that was not important to the people who designed most of the MRI machines. As a result, lots of kids are anesthetized before having a scan done. Rethinker Doug Dietz changed the outside of the MRI scanners and the uninviting clinical areas where they are located: using stickers, he turned them into pirate ships. Children who "crawl" into the "tunnel" are told to hold their breath so they don't wake up the pirates. The outcome: only 5 percent of them need anesthesia. The scene has been changed; the scan has become a game.

In IT, people traditionally work in two dimensions: *feasibility* and *viability* for the business. When they start taking account of end users, emotional needs, and business impact, there's no getting around an extra dimension. Just like with design thinking, an XLA also adds a third dimension: the user. The user becomes leading in the development, delivery, and improvement of services. Moreover, *user desirability* is at the heart of the relationship between feasibility and eventual viability. Design thinking puts the end user first in product development; an XLA puts the end user first in the provision of IT services.

START WITH AWARENESS

How do you move IT end users and their experience to the fore? How can CIOs put a stop to the excessive left-brain thinking in their IT organization? And how can you make an XLA part of IT services? Mapping the routes to the desired end user experience is a reverse step-by-step process: start with the destination and work back to the starting point. To facilitate this process (why, what, how), Giarte has developed a template, an interactive brainstorming method that offers structure and something to hold on to in the various steps that you as an IT organization can follow to draw up an XLA. The template is comparable to the Business Model Canvas, a visual method for developing new or documenting existing business models.

Every change in mentality starts with awareness and recognition. Before putting users first and gauging, analyzing, and improving their satisfaction (plan-do-check-act), the stakeholders need a common view of the experience. IT organizations need to start by recognizing the problem that users are duped by the mania for organization and pressure for processes. It's for good reason that the first part of the step-by-step plan of Alcoholics Anonymous (AA) is to admit you have a problem. Admission is also the starting point of an XLA. It helps to have a wide coalition of people who are well-disposed to change, making it important to involve a broad group. Moreover, there's a difference between developing applications (mobile apps and portals) and operational IT such as providing workplace services, application management, and infrastructure. An XLA is a major change of attitude, especially for the world of operational IT. When these services are insourced and outsourced, the stakeholders are varied: from heads of workplace management to IT purchasing agents and from legal experts to delivery managers. The good news is that this group is multidisciplinary. The less good news is that they will have rarely worked together before. With the aid of a template, however, you can develop a basis and a common view across all stakeholders.

Put a Face on the User

The first step in drawing up an XLA is to identify your customers: who your users are and what they do, think, and feel. These personas can be created through observance, experience, and collecting information, such as from customer satisfaction studies and interviews. *Personas* are characterizations of user types or internal and/or external customers, each with their own special needs and traits. The use of target groups in IT comes from the world of software development, and is meant to focus attention on the users in the design process. The IT organization also provides services to users and employees (and sometimes even business end customers and consumers), who can be placed in categories such as power workers, managers on the

XLA STATE OF MIND

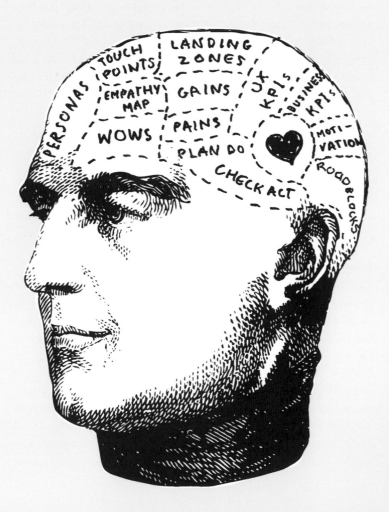

go, office workers, and field service engineers. Users are included in the drafting process by letting them talk about their experiences and pain points. By giving each persona a human name, the different user types are given a more human face for the designers. By putting itself in their position and describing their biotope, the IT organization can get to know its customers. Useful questions for determining who the persona really is and what the persona does:

- How would you describe the persona's job in 30 seconds?
- For which tasks and activities is dependency on IT the greatest?
- Which systems and functionalities are important for a typical working day?
- What are the moments of truth (peaks, days/periods) in which IT makes the difference?
- What equipment is used by the persona and in which proportions?
- Which forms of connectivity does the persona need for daily work?
- What are the persona's support preferences, assuming a mixture of channels such as telephone, chat, instant messaging, self-service, e-mail, on-site support, and a genius bar?

Pain Points and Opportunities

It is important to know not only what a persona does but also what goes on in a persona's mind. An *Empathy Map* is a simple and visual method for gaining deeper insight into customers. This interactive approach was conceived by design agency XPLANE and developed for IT organizations by Giarte. An empathy map is created for each persona to paint a clear picture of what the different personas see, think, feel, and discuss. The empathy map also includes a summary of the obstacles the persona experiences (*pains*), the needs of the persona that IT can respond to (*gains*), and the potential innovation breakthroughs (*wows*). When describing the wows, the point is to establish a connection between trends for breakthroughs in productivity and user happiness. The fast pace of innovation in IT makes new and previously unimaginable solutions possible, thereby creating the conditions for a giant leap forward. What new opportunities can be found, for example, in wearables, virtual reality, virtualization of graphical processing units, and 4G/5G for users in the field? And what opportunities are offered by trends like instant messaging bots, WebRTC for video and voice communication via web browsers, and social support between users for office personnel? The point of the wow is that the perfect trend storm does not get ignored.

The What and When of Experience

An experience itself cannot be designed – but the conditions that lead to the best possible experience can. For IT, it is important to know where and when users experience things so that can be taken into account. Experiences may relate to support channels, business processes, business applications, and the performance of systems such as access to and availability of an online work environment. These are *touchpoints* as opposed to things like a data center, database or wide area network. They exist, but users might not directly or consciously "experience" them. A compact or light-weight laptop computer, the speed of Wi-Fi, hassle-free log-in procedures, online training courses, handy applications, and an attentive response to questions or incidents: these are the things that end users do consciously experience. That experience may relate to various aspects of the specific IT service: a new version of a business application can be experienced as fast or slow, with good or bad availability, and with a long or short learning curve. Experience points can be identified for business stakeholders too, such as the delivery of important IT projects or the performance of business-critical systems. A good overview of the touchpoints enables you to decide what the desired experience should be.

Experience Landing Zones

How do you want users to look back on an incident handled by the help desk? On the delivery of a new workstation? On the rollout of a new release of a core application? Start by describing the moments of truth for the touchpoints. Preventing an extremely negative feeling at unpleasant moments (such as a system failure, late fulfillment of a request or undoing a bad application release) can be just as important as aiming for the most positive experience (such as when introducing a new application, rolling out a new workstation or launching a corporate app store). What are customers' most positive experiences and which experiences lead to the most dissatisfaction? A reality check is performed by placing circles around the different IT services (from "excited" in the middle to "happy," "okay," "who cares," "frustrated," and "angry") and then describing the desired experience in the "landing zone." So why are you unable to create the desired experience?

List the Conditional Yeses

What's stopping you from delivering the desired experience with the existing processes, rules, and KPIs? Zoom out and look at the obstacles in the processes and behavior. Why is the customer experience still frequently sub-optimal or sometimes even bad? The reason often lies in a contract that covers all the wrong things, unnecessarily complex processes, perverse control parameters or micromanaging the vendors – which of course is counterproductive. These "conditional yeses" sometimes reflect painfully on the vendor IT organizations and chains with multiple players, such as in the case of multivendor outsourcing. Why is it so hard to achieve a high score for satisfaction? And what can we do about that? This step is about eliminating things "that are just the way they are," "that have always been the deal" or other arguments in the "conditional yes" category. Does everyone agree that these obstacles exist, without immediately falling back into pointing out the causes?

A good way to open up obstacles for discussion with humor is to make a not-to-do list. What are we going to stop doing because there's no point to it anymore, creates negative energy or is counter-productive? What are we going to see from now on as a CWOT (Complete Waste of Time)? Just ask these questions in a workshop and watch the floodgates open. After all, who hasn't had to deal with time-consuming reports, unnecessary meetings, perverse KPIs, and vague projects without any clear objective?

For an interactive session such as a workshop, the Cool Wall is a great troubleshooter. The Cool Wall in TV show *Top Gear* is covered with pictures of cars arranged into four categories of coolness: "seriously uncool," "uncool," "cool," and "sub-zero." By placing applications, projects, departments, scorecards, and other visible artifacts of IT on a Cool Wall, you can lower the threshold to talk about things that a lot of your co-workers also have an opinion about. This informal setting creates openness.

Formulate Meaningful KPIs

What does the KPI framework look like when the end user experience occupies center stage? When putting end users and the business organization first, some KPIs will have to be replaced by KPIs reflecting the impact on the business and users. But if you start pulling the plug on the old KPI model out of nowhere, you can expect some resistance. That's why it's a good idea to assess the existing KPIs first to see whether all the KPIs really are KPIs. The litmus test for a KPI is the answer to the question whether the KPI is a measure of the success of the business. KPIs are used (and misused) too often to demonstrate performance. An XLA simplifies the KPI models; the number of indicators is reduced, and those that remain paint a better picture of what is actually important for the business organization and users. The past years, the Net Promoter Score (NPS) has successfully established itself as the KPI for customer satisfaction. The NPS shows how likely customers are to recommend a company or organization. The NPS is often used along with a Customer Effort Score (CES), which measures how much personal effort it takes a customer to get a company to do something. An IT variant of the Customer Effort Score is the *No Hassle* KPI: how much hassle does it take an IT end user to get the service provider to do something?

MENTAL ROADMAP

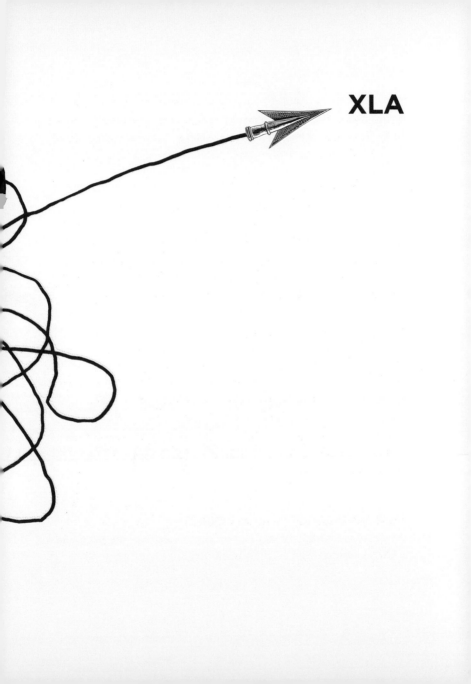

XLA

That "something" can be resolving an incident, providing a service from a catalog, answering a question, handling a complaint, etc. This KPI is indirectly an indicator of waste: the greater the hassle, the less value is added in the view of the IT end user.

Use the Right Motivation

In essence, an XLA is all about teamwork, openness, and the intrinsic will to make improvements on a constant basis. That's not possible in an environment where carrots and sticks – the most primitive form of motivation – are leading. Yet that is how traditional thinking in IT organizations works. The biggest disadvantage of traditional SLAs is the CYA culture that often dominates: everyone just tries to cover their own ass, with little regard for what happens in the rest of the chain. The reasons for dissatisfaction need to be brought out into the open. How are incentives used to keep motivating people to go the extra mile? It's not extrinsic motivation (punishment, reward) but, instead, intrinsic motivation (pride, passion) that makes the difference in getting people to commit to doing their best. KPIs for punctuality (on-time flight departures or correctly filled orders) or contextual availability (no negative effect on sales or customer satisfaction) ensure that everyone in the supply chain can feel responsible for the final result.

USER SATISFACTION IN HARD FIGURES

When going through the steps for an XLA, measuring user satisfaction takes on another dimension. When IT organizations gauge their own customer satisfaction, this is often a low-frequency measurement without any clear relationship to learning or improving. With an XLA, that measurement of experience goes deeper and is more specific. Companies that start using an XLA take a fresh look at the provision of IT services and use other KPIs to monitor other goals: the impact of the quality of IT on the business organization and end users. The combination of perception data and data relating to the technical performance of systems and IT service management enables them to find connections and work towards continuous improvement. In advanced forms of user experience monitoring, use is also made of open comments from surveys taken by IT end users for social buzz and sentiment analyses.

It takes more than the measurement and smart analysis of data on user experiences to stimulate the empathy of IT professionals; a physical dialog needs to be opened up with the users as well. More and more IT organizations rely on user panels to gather feedback. For instance, Rabobank regularly hosts IT user panels with a moderator where IT professionals are only allowed to observe. The users provide feedback on what they experience and give advice on what they would like to be done differently in the area of IT services.

MILLENNIALS SPEED UP THE SWITCH TO XLAS

My 13-year-old daughter wears a T-shirt that says "Don't steal my Wi-Fi." In her experience, technology is not made up of "things"; technology stands for a lifestyle. Saying things like "My computer doesn't feel like working," "My iPhone is so cute," or "Wi-Fi lets me down" shows that users ascribe human traits to the technology that they use. Known as anthropomorphism, this phenomenon is on the rise.

In the run-up to 2020, we will see the number of *digital natives* increase and the number of *digital immigrants* decrease. In that year, Generation Y (born in the 1980s and 1990s) will make up nearly half of the average human resources. The other half will be made up of their predecessors: people who experienced the rise of the computer (Generation X) and those who lived through the reconstruction and democratization of trade and industry (baby boomers). Where the baby boomers still believed in collectivism and solidarity, people from Generations Y and Z attach increasing importance to individualism. The youngest generation of employees have a different view of industrial relations, ways of working and communicating, technology, and the balance between work and private life. They have been raised with IT consumerization and make no distinction between themselves as private individuals and as users of business IT. Millennials are completely *tech savvy*: heavy users in their private life. In addition, people from Generation Y and Z have a problem with having everything decided for them and dictated from above. They want to make their own choices. Increasingly, they place *purpose* above *profit*.

In regards to IT, Millennials are mainly interested in convenience and functionality: IT as an effective and efficient means for them to achieve their goal. Young IT end users are inventive, self-reliant,

MILLENNIAL MASLOW

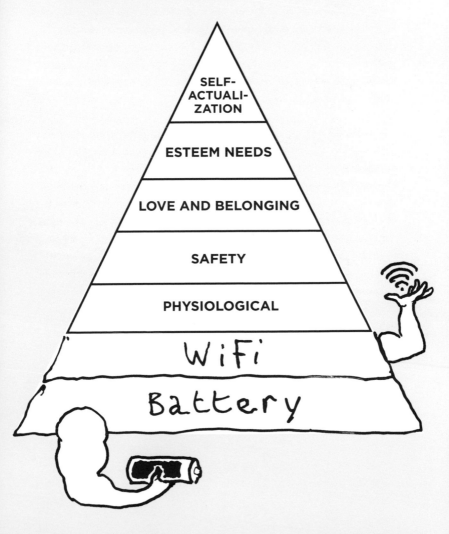

and discerning. If a solution is not good enough, they will see it as a bad solution and look for an alternative. Generation Y and Z are therefore not particularly loyal to brands, products or services. In their job, a feeling of fulfillment and purpose is more important than a traditional career; fluid forms of collaboration, where teams, times and locations are determined as needed, are preferred to fixed patterns of working.

Apple, Facebook, Spotify, and Airbnb were all founded by people in their twenties. They might be a little older now, but they are real Millennials: completely comfortable with technology and no big fans of a traditional career in business. And most important, besides being so sure of themselves, so in command, they also created a generation of IT users who are equally sure of themselves, equally in command. These are the people we as leaders and managers, also in IT, will have to deal with increasingly in the years to come. For all these people, IT is not a side issue – it is a major issue. For us as IT professionals, effective collaboration with them is crucial.

"Start with the customer experience and work back towards the technology."

Steve Jobs
1955 - 2011

And here's why not to go XLA:

1

It is harder to stand out than it is to fit in.
You will have to win some hearts.

2

It is a work in progress.
You will build the plane while flying it.

3

It has no certification program.
There will be no training points awarded.

ACKNOWLEDGEMENTS

You pick up a book, you read the story and you put it down. Nobody ever really reads the acknowledgements. So if you stumble upon this page and find yourself reading this, I thank you for showing interest.

Nothing is ever really done. With any new idea, you always feel the urge to leave things unfinished. This book is my promise to shape and define my ideas about of what I call: the eXperience Level Agreement. I wanted it to be brief and easy to read, and to encourage people to change direction in enterprise IT. I would like to express my gratitude to those who influenced, inspired and helped me: Saul van Beurden, Henk Boon, Joe Ciancio, Martin Curley, Henk Gianotten, Reinout Jörg, Brian Johnson, Michiel ten Kate, Jo Krill, Niels Loader, Alan Nance, Ronald Paans, Paul Piebinga, Isabella Prins, Sven van de Riet, Linda Lyklema, Leon-Paul de Rouw, Martin Schoonheim, Michiel Valk, Jeroen Tas, Wouter Keller, Paul Iske, and Frans van der Reep.

And last but not least; I ask for compassion for all those who have been working with me in the course of the years and whose names I have failed to mention.

NOTES

1. Pettey, C. (2010). *Gartner Estimates Global "IT Debt" to Be $500 Billion This Year, with Potential to Grow to $1 Trillion by 2015.* Gartner at http://www.gartner.com/newsroom/id/1439513

2. Gazzaniga, M.S., Bogen, J.E. & Sperry, R.W. (1962). *Some functional effects of sectioning the cerebral commissures in man.* Proceedings of the National Academy of Sciences of the United States of America at http://www.pnas.org/content/48/10/1765

3. Zollo, M. (2013). *The innovative brain.* MIT Management Sloan School at http://mitsloanexperts.mit.edu/the-innovative-brain-maurizio-zollo/

4. Williams Woolley, A., Chabris, C.F., Pentland, A., Hashmi, N. & Malone, T.W. (2010). *Evidence for a Collective Intelligence Factor in the Performance of Human Groups.* Science at http://science.sciencemag.org/content/330/6004/686

5. Sinek, S. (2014). *Leaders Eat Last: Why Some Teams Pull Together and Others Don't.* London: Penguin Random House

6. Pink, D.H. (2006). *A Whole New Mind: Why Right-Brainers Will Rule the Future.* New York: Riverhead Books

7. Mintzberg, H. (2001). *Why I Hate Flying: Tales for the Tormented Traveler.* Cheshire: Texere Publishing

8. Sinek, S. (2011). *Start With Why: How Great Leaders Inspire Everyone To Take Action.* London: Penguin Random House

9. Skinner, B.F. (1938). *The Behavior of Organisms: An Experimental Analysis.* New York: Appleton-Century

10. Luyendijk, J. (2015). *Swimming with Sharks: My Journey Into the World of the Bankers.* London: Guardian Faber

11. Anders, G. (2013). *The Number One Job Skill in 2020.* LinkedIn at https://www.linkedin.com/pulse/20130611180041-59549-the-no-1-job-skill-in-2020

READING LIST

Tips from the author:

- Araujo, C. (2012). *The Quantum Age of IT: Why Everything You Know About IT Is About To Change*. Cambridgeshire: IT Governance

- Frankl, V.E. & Winslade, W.J. (2004). *A Man's Search For Meaning*. London: Rider Books (an imprint of Ebury Publishing)

- Gawande, A. (2011). *The Checklist Manifesto: How To Get Things Right*. London: Profile Books LTD

- Glen, P. (2003). *Leading Geeks: How To Manage and Lead People Who Deliver Technology*. San Francisco: John Wiley & Sons

- Kim, G., Behr, K. & Spafford, G. (2013). *The Phoenix Project: A Novel About IT, DevOps, and Helping Your Business Win*. Portland: IT Revolution Press

- Pink, D.H. (2005). *A Whole New Mind: Why Right-Brainers Will Rule the Future*. New York: Riverhead Books

- Pink, D.H. (2009). *Drive: The Surprising Truth About What Motivates Us*. New York: Riverhead Books

- Sinek, S. (2011). *Start With Why: How Great Leaders Inspire Everyone to Take Action*. London: Penguin Books Ltd.

- Sinek, S. (2014). *Leaders Eat Last: Why Some Teams Pull Together and Others Don't*. London: Penguin Books Ltd.

- Stickdorn, M. & Schneider J. (2011). *This is Service Design Thinking: Basics – Tools – Cases*. Amsterdam: BIS publishers

- Wood, J.B., Hewlin, T. & Lah, T. (2013). B4B: *How Technology and Big Data Are Reinventing the Customer-Supplier Relationship*. San Diego: Tsia

INDEX

Visit **www.digitalempathy.rocks** for more information about this publication, lectures, and materials to get started with eXperience Level Agreements. Visit www.giarte.com for more information about the method, advice, and tools that Giarte provides companies and the public sector to make the difference in managing and improving IT.